DISASTER RECOVERY PLANNING

EXPLANATORY NOTE AND CASE STUDY

JUNE 2023

ASIAN DEVELOPMENT BANK

ADB

ISBN 978-92-9270-143-7 (print); 978-92-9270-144-4 (electronic); 978-92-9270-145-1 (ebook)
Publication Stock No. TIM230163-2
DOI: http://dx.doi.org/10.22617/TIM230163-2

Notes:
In this publication, "$" refers to United States dollars.
In this publication, tables, figures, and maps without explicit sources are those of the authors.

This publication was prepared in May 2023 by the Sustainable Development and Climate Change Department based on the draft technical report submitted by post-disaster needs assessment expert and consultant Roberto Jovel.

Cover photo: **Earthquake Emergency Assistance Project in Nepal.** A woman from Singla village extracts her belongings from the rubble (photo by ADB).

Cover design by Ross Locsin Laccay.

Contents

Tables and Figure

TABLES

FIGURE

Acknowledgments

The *Disaster Recovery Planning: Explanatory Note and Case Study* was prepared by the Climate Change and Disaster Risk Management Division of the Sustainable Development and Climate Change Department of the Asian Development Bank (ADB).

Steven Goldfinch, senior disaster risk management specialist, provided overall guidance in the development of the publication supported by Anne Orquiza, senior public management officer (Disaster Risk Management). Roberto Jovel (post-disaster needs assessment expert, ADB consultant) led the development of the technical publication. Melanie Kelleher and Margie Peters-Fawcett (ADB consultants) edited the publication, and Rocilyn Locsin Laccay (ADB contractor) provided graphics and layout.

The publication benefited from peer reviews and detailed comments from the following Climate Change and Disaster Risk Management Division staff: Charlotte Benson, principal disaster risk management specialist; Belinda Hewitt, senior disaster risk management specialist; Brigitte Balthasar, senior disaster risk and climate risk financing specialist, and Sifayet Mohammad Ullah, disaster risk management specialist.

National Flood Emergency Response in Pakistan. Children play on a railway damaged by the Pakistan floods of September 2010 (photo by ADB).

Explanatory Note

1.   Introduction

A post-disaster needs assessment (PDNA) aims to assess the full extent of the impact of a disaster on a country and—based on its findings—produce an actionable and sustainable recovery strategy to mobilize financial and technical resources. If necessary, a PDNA will also request additional external cooperation and assistance for implementation, depending on the financial, technical, and institutional capacities of a country.[1]

A PDNA should be designed to estimate the value of financial requirements to achieve recovery and reconstruction after a disaster. Guidelines have been developed, expanded, and refined using the initial methodology developed by the United Nations Economic Commission for Latin America and the Caribbean for the assessment of the value of destroyed physical assets and losses in the production of goods and services, and the formulation of the first PDNA Handbook.[2] This process required quantitative and evidence-based information. However, the procedure to systematically and quantitatively estimate the required financial needs to achieve recovery and reconstruction has lagged. One significant development was a 2015 World Bank proposal for using a recovery framework to guide post-disaster activities for recovery and reconstruction.[3]

Quantitative procedures for the estimation of the value of financial requirements only have been described in the guidance notes of the World Bank´s Global Facility for Disaster Reduction and Recovery. These notes served to estimate recovery and reconstruction needs as of 2010.[4] This note draws from the facility's guidance notes and from field experience acquired during many post-disaster assessments to provide comprehensive and quantitative procedures for the estimation of recovery and reconstruction financial requirements following disasters of any type, using as inputs the values of damage and losses arising from the PDNA.

2.   Definition of Recovery and Reconstruction

The United Nations General Assembly adopted the definition of recovery as "The restoring or improving of livelihoods and health, as well as economic, physical, social, cultural and environmental assets, systems and activities, of a disaster-affected community or society, aligning with the principles of sustainable development and 'build back better,' to avoid or reduce future disaster risk."[5]

Further, the General Assembly adopted the definition of reconstruction as "the medium- and long-term rebuilding and sustainable restoration of resilient critical infrastructures, services, housing, facilities and livelihoods required for the full functioning of a community or a society affected by a disaster, aligning with the principles of sustainable development and 'build back better,' to avoid or reduce future disaster risk" (footnote 5).

BUILD BACK BETTER

The use of the recovery, rehabilitation, and reconstruction phases after a disaster to increase the resilience of nations and communities through integrating disaster risk reduction measures into the restoration of physical infrastructure and societal systems, and into the revitalization of livelihoods, economies, and the environment (footnote 5).

[1]   European Union, Global Facility for Disaster Reduction and Recovery, and World Bank. 2013. *Post-Disaster Needs Assessments Guidelines, Volume A*.

[2]   United Nations Economic Commission for Latin America and the Caribbean. 1991. *Manual para la estimación de los efectos socioeconómicos de los desastres naturales*, Santiago de Chile, 1991; and United Nations Economic Commission for Latin America and the Caribbean. 2003. *Handbook for the estimation of the socio-economic and environmental effects of disasters*, Mexico City.

[3]   Global Facility for Disaster Risk Reduction and The World Bank. 2015. *Guide to Developing Post-Disaster Recovery Frameworks*. Washington, DC.

[4]   R. Jovel and M. Mudahar. 2010. *Damage, Loss and Needs Assessment Guidance Notes, Volume 3, Estimation of Post-Disaster Needs for Recovery and Reconstruction*. World Bank and Global Facility for Disaster Risk Reduction. Washington, DC.

[5]   United Nations. 2017. *Report of the Open-ended Intergovernmental Expert Working Group on Indicators and Terminology Relating to Disaster Risk Reduction*. New York.

Figure: Grouping of Recovery and Reconstruction Activities

1 Reconstruction of infrastructure and physical assets.	2 Resumption of service delivery and access to goods and services.	3 Restoration of governance.	4 Risk reduction and building back better.
The value of damage and costs (quality improvement, technological modernization, disaster risk reduction features, and multi-annual inflation).	Additional costs to service providers to restore basic services and additional costs to the affected population to access services.	Additional human resources with improved capacities of service providers to undertake recovery; replacing lost records and upgrading documents of public services.	Addressing immediate risks, upgrading preparedness measures, further studies or assessments, and needs to build back better.

Note: Reconstruction constitutes the physical part of recovery. The use of the term "recovery" in this report includes the component of reconstruction.
Source: Author.

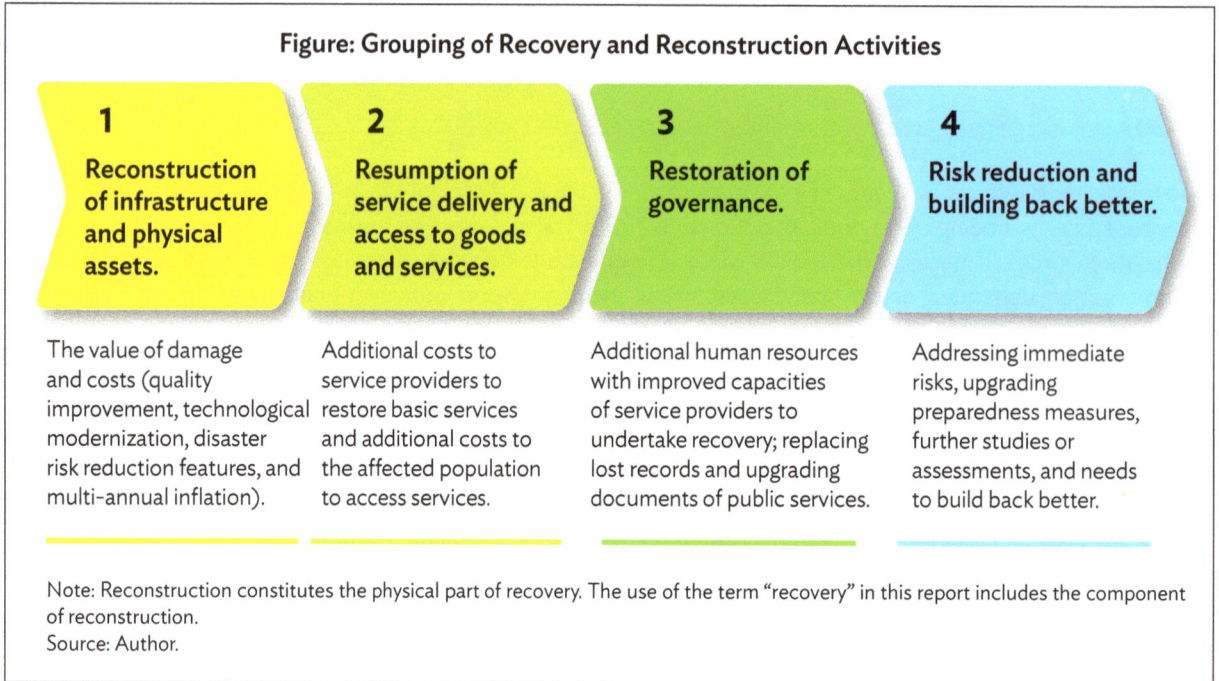

There are some misconceptions in recovery which must be identified and avoided during a PDNA to ensure proper identification of recovery and reconstruction needs. They are briefly outlined in this report.

Housing sector recovery is not achieved when temporary or emergency shelter is provided to households whose housing unit has been destroyed; rather, recovery is only reached when destroyed housing units have been rebuilt and when destroyed household goods have been replaced. Transport sector recovery is only achieved when destroyed road sectors and vehicles have been rebuilt and replaced; not when minimum traffic flows have been enabled. Health sector recovery is not complete when emergency or tent hospitals and clinics have been installed, but only when health infrastructure has been rebuilt and reequipped, and when higher rates of morbidity have been controlled and brought down to pre-disaster levels. Agriculture sector recovery is only achieved when the next crop is harvested, and the pre-disaster level of production has been obtained; not when seeds and other inputs are delivered to farmers so that they may replant their crops. Energy sector recovery is not reached when electricity flows are restored in the power grid, but when sales of electricity by the power company are back to at least pre-disaster levels. Education sector recovery is achieved when the full number of students are attending classes in the classrooms that have been rebuilt; not when tent classrooms and other alternative facilities are rented to restart education activities. Similar examples may be stated to cover all possibly affected sectors of activity.

Therefore, members of PDNA teams should estimate the amounts of financing required to achieve recovery. This means the amount of financing required to bring things to at least the same pre-disaster level of development in the affected areas.

It is essential to realize that the time to achieve recovery will be different among different sectors of economic and social activity—depending on the degree of disaster effects and impact sustained—and that overall recovery may be reached only when all affected sectors and people have overcome the effects and impacts of the disaster. The time required for recovery after each disaster will vary depending on the hazard and intensity, geographic coverage, and extent to which each sector was affected. As of 2023, no criteria exist to define such a timeframe.

3.   Requirements of the Estimation of Damage and Losses

The identification of recovery and reconstruction needs within a PDNA is made based on the results of the estimation of disaster effects—which include damage and losses—and of the analysis of the disaster impact at the macroeconomic, sector, and household levels.

The term "damage" refers to the value of fully or partially destroyed physical assets and infrastructure, using the unit cost of construction that prevailed in the affected area before the disaster occurred. The term "losses" refers to the value of changes in economic flows that arise after the disaster strikes: the decline in the value of the production of goods and services and the value of possible higher costs of production. In a PDNA, disaster effects (damage and losses) are estimated for all sectors of economic and social activity in the disaster-affected areas, and use is made of the globally adopted system of national accounts for such estimations to standardize results.[6]

After the effects of a disaster have been estimated, this value is used to measure the macroeconomic disaster impact to ascertain their consequences on the development of the affected country, for which the use of the standardized system of national accounts—in terms of the definition of sectors of economic and social activities and their boundaries—is essential. A disaster may harm overall economic growth, the balance of trade and balance of payments (BOP), and the fiscal performance of a country. The ensuing need to recover the previous levels of development can then be estimated.

In addition to the macroeconomic analysis, estimates of personal or household disaster impacts should be made to determine the negative disaster effects on social and welfare conditions and to estimate financial requirements for their recovery. PDNA estimations of the value of damage and losses—which constitutes the basis for the quantitative estimation of recovery needs—must conform to some uniform requirements:

(i) **Assessments should cover the estimation of all destroyed physical assets (damage), losses in the production of goods and services, and possible post-disaster higher costs of production, whether such activities are owned privately or by the public sector.** In some cases, assessments conducted cover only—or mostly—damage and losses to government-owned facilities and services. This is because it is erroneously assumed that private individuals and enterprises have savings and/or insurance that will enable private sector recovery. This assumption cannot be readily adopted in the case of disasters that occur in developing countries where insurance coverage is often very limited and private savings are usually scarce. Making such an assumption would result in only parts of the affected areas and individuals eventually achieving a return to pre-disaster levels of development, and that a sizable part of the economy and population—represented by private ownership—would not receive the benefit of recovery investments and support. In addition, the negative impact of the disaster at the macroeconomic level would prevent or delay overall recovery, and human suffering would be higher and longer for part of the population.

Another alleged reason for covering only publicly owned damage and losses in a PDNA may be the erroneous belief that the affected government is only interested in learning the financial requirements for reconstruction and recovery that falls within its direct domain. Governments need to know the total amount of recovery and reconstruction financing that is required to maintain at least the same level of macroeconomic performance prevailing before a disaster, and the amounts required for recovery and reconstruction of private assets and activities through the banking system and capital markets.

(ii) **The assessment should include all sectors of economic and social activity that may have sustained damage and losses because of the disaster, not just the more affected sectors.** If recovery and reconstruction needs are estimated based on a partial coverage assessment, full recovery will not be achieved because of the normal

---

[6]   The list and scope of sectors of economic and social activity in a PDNA are to be defined on the basis of the System of National Accounts and not by the names and institutional scope of the agencies that participate in the assessment of disaster effects.

interaction between sectors, and parts of the affected population will suffer limitations. The extent and boundaries of all sectors of activity—defined in the system of national accounts that all countries have—must be respected when estimating damage and losses. Otherwise, the subsequent analysis of disaster impact at the macroeconomic level will be faulty and possibly under- or overestimated.

In some previous PDNAs, damage and losses of pharmaceutical industries have been erroneously included as part of the health sector, and disaster effects on selected agroindustrial establishments have been included as part of the agriculture sector. Using such erroneous data as input for the macroeconomic impact analysis is wrong, as the weight in the value of the gross domestic product of each sector—as defined in the system of national accounts—is different. Therefore, the scope and boundaries of each sector should always follow the definitions provided in the national accounts.

(iii) **The estimation of the value of destroyed physical assets should be based on prevailing unit construction costs in the affected area, and the characteristics or capacity of the destroyed assets just before or at the time of the disaster.** It will then be possible to ascertain the replacement costs of destroyed assets, which form the basis for validly estimating reconstruction needs. After the correct estimation of the value of damage using these criteria, reconstruction requirements should be estimated by introducing risk-reduction coefficients.

(iv) **A special sample survey of the industry and commerce sectors should be undertaken to collect sample data on damage, losses, and recovery needs for a limited number of sample enterprises.**

(v) **To avoid double or multiple accounting, care should be exercised not to include personal income losses in the total amount of damage and losses.** Since labor costs are already included in the production cost, the inclusion of personal income losses in total losses would constitute clear double accounting. PDNA team members should realize that personal income losses are estimated only to understand disaster impact on households and will be used to estimate possible personal or household income recovery needs that will be deducted from sector production recovery needs.

4.   Procedures to Estimate Recovery and Reconstruction Needs

The PDNA is a unitary process that includes the quantification of disaster effects and impacts at the sector, macro, and micro levels of analysis; after which the values of damage and losses are used as inputs to estimate the amounts of financing required to achieve recovery and reconstruction. Specifically, recovery financing requirements must be estimated as a function of the values of the changes in the flows of the economy and the decline in personal or household income arising from the disaster, and reconstruction requirements estimated as a function of the value of destroyed or damaged physical assets.

Recovery needs in the productive sectors of agriculture, manufacturing, trade, mining, and tourism are, in fact, the amounts of working capital that producers require to achieve recovery of production levels. The needs for recovery in service sectors—including education, health, culture, transport and communications, energy, and water and sanitation—are the amounts of financing required, over and above regular budget appropriations, to restore supply and access to the affected population. Estimations of personal or household income decline from the drop in production at sector levels can be used to define possible temporary financial requirements to assist the affected population (through cash-for-work schemes or other similar income assistance programs) until they are independent. Reconstruction requirements—or physical recovery—are estimated based on the value of destroyed assets, supplemented to introduce risk-reduction standards.

The total value of disaster effects (i.e., damage and losses) is not equal to the value of recovery and reconstruction needs. Recovery needs are normally equivalent to a fraction of the estimated losses in sector production and supplemented with the possible higher cost of production following the disaster after deducting possible insurance proceeds that producers may have. Reconstruction needs are usually higher than the estimated value of destroyed assets as they are often rebuilt at higher standards to reduce disaster risk. The increases in unit construction costs adopted for the estimation of reconstruction needs will depend not only on the pre-disaster design standards but also on the degree of disaster resilience desired. Over many years, the average increase in unit costs for different sectors has been recorded and is used as a guide for the estimation of reconstruction needs.

5.   Estimation of Recovery Needs in Productive Sectors

Following a disaster, it is essential to restore production levels to the productive sectors. During the initial stage of the PDNA, an estimation is made of the value of the production of goods that are unavailable because of the disruption caused by the disaster. This production economic loss cannot be replaced. Production recovery needs to refer to the amount of working capital required by the producers (i.e., individuals or enterprises) or to the necessary inputs required to restore production levels.

Agriculture

Agriculture normally includes subsectors of crop production, livestock, and fisheries. In the **crops subsector**, recovery of production usually involves the provision of inputs required for planting the next crop, which the producers may not have after the disaster. The value of production **recovery needs** in the case of annual crops may be estimated as a fraction of the value of production lost, which ranges from 18% to 26%, depending on the type of crop involved. An agronomist or agricultural economist can quantify these values using statistical information available in all countries (footnote 4).

In the case where a disaster may have destroyed permanent trees and crops, production will not be restored to normal levels until the trees have been replanted and grown to maturity, so that they may begin producing again. This will involve the cost of replanting the trees—perhaps using varieties that are more resilient to the impact of disasters—which can be viewed as the reconstruction of the destroyed assets, and the cost of nurturing the new plants until maturity. In some cases, production will be lost over 3–6 years, depending on the kind of fruit trees involved. An agronomist or agricultural economist will be able to define such costs and growth periods.

Crop **reconstruction needs** should be estimated to replace any physical durable assets that may have been destroyed (e.g., agriculture-related buildings—including storage facilities—agricultural machinery, fences, irrigation and drainage works, and permanent plantations) and their corresponding value is calculated based on the estimated damage figure, increased by a certain percentage to allow for the introduction of disaster risk reduction features. Increments of damage from 25% to 35% have been found, depending on the pre-disaster standards of design and construction (footnote 4).

Livestock subsector **recovery needs** are estimated as a function of the possible requirements of prevention and control of animal disease that may arise following a disaster to avoid negatively affecting the future supply of meat and other food derivatives from domestic animals, as well as the lack of sufficient traction force for the sector when animals are used for such purposes. In cases of drought or other disasters that have an impact on supply chains, animal feed and watering costs also may have to be provided to ensure recovery of the animal stock. The cost of such recovery needs can be estimated by a veterinarian and other livestock experts based on statistical information available in the affected country.

Depending on the severity of the death rate of domestic animals caused by the disaster—as well as the resulting food deficit—the value of replacing the animal stock may be included as a reconstruction need, rather than allowing the natural rate of animal growth to take its course. In this case, the value of damage to the animal stock may be increased by a certain percentage to enable the acquisition of animal varieties that are more resistant to drought or other hazards.

In the **fisheries** and **aquaculture subsector**, the cost of destroyed or damaged infrastructure (including ponds, boats, nets and other gear, docking, and storage facilities, as well as fingerling stock) should be increased by 25% to 35% to allow for **reconstruction needs** that have disaster-resilient features. Recovery needs refer to the amount of working capital that fisherfolk require to restart and conduct normal operations and are a function of the value of lost production at around 15%–25%.

The loss of production in the entire agriculture sector caused by a disaster may result in food insecurity or food deficits for the affected population and income reduction and deficits of the affected households until required to recover normalcy in production and personal or household income levels. In these cases, special programs of **temporary food supply or income support** may have to be implemented, which costs are to be defined based on the estimated value of foodstuff lost or of personal or household income decline, including the cost of transport of the alternative sources of food.

Mining

The mining sector—in some cases referred to as the mining and quarrying sector—normally includes the extraction of minerals as well as the extraction of oil and gas. After a disaster, **recovery needs** in this sector may include the cost of pumping flood waters from flooded mines; the cost of shoring up tunnels and other parts of mines that have sustained partial damage; the cost of removing equipment and materials from disaster-affected areas of oil and gas fields; the possible higher-than-normal cost of operating alternative oil and gas production units that replace extraction in damaged or destroyed units; the cost of cleaning up spilled mine tailings and spilled oil in adjacent areas; and the possible cost of drilling emergency oil and gas wells to expedite recovery of supply.

Reconstruction needs should be estimated by taking the damage value and increasing it to ensure the introduction of enhanced disaster risk reduction standards. There is no standardized factor to achieve such improved resilience, as few cases of disaster in the mining field have been assessed and documented.

Frequently, mining enterprises in this sector will have insurance coverage for the destruction of assets and lost revenues. After estimates have been made of gross recovery and reconstruction needs, the value of such insurance proceeds should be deducted to arrive at a net value of needs.

Manufacturing

Post-disaster **recovery needs** for the industry or manufacturing sector are defined as the amounts of financing required to ensure that production returns to at least pre-disaster levels of performance. Recovery needs for the sector may include the availability of credit to finance the working capital required to recommence enterprise operations which—in turn—may require financing to reschedule nonperforming loans arising from the disaster, as well as the possible higher cost of operations after the disaster. During the PDNA stage of assessing disaster effects for this sector, industry owners or managers should be questioned about needs they may have already identified.

The amount of required working capital and possibly higher cost of operation in the manufacturing sector after a disaster are equivalent to 25%–45% of the value of production loss. Industrial economists in the PDNA team should be able to define the percentage value to be adopted in each case of disaster, using information obtained during interviews and field surveys with industry owners or managers in the affected areas, as well as on the size and type of the manufacturing process involved.

The industry or manufacturing sector may be run by private enterprises or publicly owned industries that may or may not have disaster insurance on assets and production. Recovery financing need not be provided solely by the government to all affected enterprises but could be by a combination of government and private banks; and offered under softer-than-usual terms given the extraordinary situation brought about by the disaster. As such, recovery financing for this sector may include a combination of alternative channels such as cash grants to microenterprises, soft-term credit to small- to medium-sized enterprises, and possible temporary tax-relief schemes for larger industrial enterprises.

Reconstruction needs for the manufacturing sector are determined based on the estimated value of destroyed physical assets augmented by a certain fraction to provide for increased disaster-resilient standards. These cost increases can range from 25% to 35% of the value of the damage.

After estimating the value of recovery and reconstruction needs for the manufacturing sector, estimated proceeds from insurance schemes on destroyed assets and production losses must be deducted to arrive at the net value of post-disaster needs for the sector.

Commerce

The estimation of post-disaster needs for the commerce or trade sector follows closely those of the industry or manufacturing sector. It also relies on data collected through the sample survey.

Recovery needs for the commerce sector are estimated based on the capital requirements for individual traders or enterprises to maintain an adequate flow of goods to sell, as the disaster may have destroyed their stock of goods for sale. Multiple assessments conclude that traders require working capital—depending on the size and type of commerce units—of 20%–35% of the normal value of sales. Trade economists in the PDNA team covering the commerce sector should be able to estimate the most appropriate percentage to be adopted using data collected during the field sample survey as well as information obtained during interviews with commerce unit owners and managers.

In the commerce sector, most trade activities may lie in the hands of private sector enterprises or individuals as well as the public sector. Some of the enterprises may have insurance on lost revenue as well as on the physical assets that are required for their trade activities. In the field survey, data on the source of financing of these trade establishments (e.g., supplier credit, family remittances from abroad, savings, etc.) should be collected and used to define post-disaster working capital requirements.

As with the manufacturing sector, total sector recovery needs should be estimated, but the government should not be required to provide sector-wide post-disaster financial support. The government could provide targeted assistance such as cash grants for the recapitalization of micro traders, guide the private banking system in providing soft-term recovery financing to the rest of the sector entrepreneurs, and—in some cases—provide temporary tax relief to most-affected traders.

Reconstruction needs for the commerce sector are determined based on the estimated value of destroyed physical assets, augmented by a certain fraction to provide for increased disaster-resilient standards. These cost increases range from 25% to 35% of the value of the damage.

After estimating the value of recovery and reconstruction needs for the commerce sector, estimated proceeds from insurance schemes on destroyed assets and production losses must be deducted to arrive at the net value of post-disaster needs for the sector.

Tourism

In many cases, due to its importance in generating employment and foreign revenues—as is the case for many small island developing countries—the tourism sector is covered separately from the commerce sector.

Recovery needs in this sector include not only the recapitalization of tourism enterprises after a disaster but—most importantly—promotional activities to recapture foreign and domestic tourists who may have ceased arriving in the affected country or area affected by the disaster. During interviews undertaken by the assessment team with tourism sector representatives and owners, the cost of such promotional activities must be ascertained to supplement the need to ensure the availability of working capital in the same fashion as in the case of the commerce sector. The government may be required to cofinance such a promotional campaign as part of its efforts to stabilize macroeconomic balances.

The recovery process may include the provision by the private banking system of special credit lines for the recapitalization of small- to medium-sized hotels and restaurants, as well as possible tax relief measures. To estimate such financial requirements, the PDNA tourism sector team should analyze data on sources of financing that sector entrepreneurs may have available to them such as savings, insurance proceeds, and other possible sources such as remittances from abroad.

Reconstruction needs should be estimated in the same manner as described for other sectors; by increasing the estimated value of damage by 25%–35% to provide for enhanced disaster risk reduction standards.

Once recovery and reconstruction needs have been estimated, the tourism sector PDNA team should deduct the estimated value of available insurance proceeds on destroyed assets and on revenue losses to arrive at the net value of needs for the sector.

6.   Estimation of Recovery Needs in Services Sectors

After a disaster, it is essential to restore supply and consumer access in the service sectors of education, health, housing, energy, water supply, and sanitation, transport, and communications.

Education

After a disaster occurs, education infrastructure and materials are destroyed, and education services are disrupted. As a result, classes may be discontinued for a relatively long period and students of different levels are directly affected.

Recovery needs include the cost of replacement of education materials; alternative rented premises to reinitiate classes, when required; compensation of lost teaching time and any additional non-teaching hours for teachers and other staff; and psycho-social counseling to assist students in overcoming the impact of the disaster.

Reconstruction needs for destroyed infrastructure are estimated as a function of the value of damage, increased by 10%–25% to enhance disaster-risk reduction standards. In addition, partially damaged infrastructure must be retrofitted to ensure they conform to the same enhanced standards of design.

Estimated insurance policy proceeds should be deducted from the estimated gross value of recovery and reconstruction needs to arrive at their net value.

Health

The health sector is usually affected by disasters, not only in terms of the destruction of its infrastructure and the disruptions of its normal services but also because of the increased workload to attend to the affected population, either because of injuries or due to higher morbidity rates arising from unfavorable post-disaster conditions.

Recovery needs may include the cost of (i) providing health care to affected individuals during the emergency, which are over and above the normal budgetary levels of the sector; (ii) the setting up and operation of temporary health facilities required to rebuild destroyed infrastructure; (iii) the replacement of health materials and supplies used during the emergency; and (iv) the monitoring and eventual control of possible disease outbreaks arising from modified environmental conditions brought about by the disaster (e.g., vector control, disease prevention, and medical attention to sick patients). Two other possible cases of post-disaster recovery needs include the cost of disposal of hospital waste and nutrition treatment of children and other vulnerable population groups if the disaster leads to food insecurity.

Reconstruction needs involve the estimation of the reconstruction cost for destroyed infrastructure plus the higher cost of enhanced disaster risk reduction standards to their new design, as well as the retrofitting of partially damaged infrastructure to conform to the same. The increased cost may range from 10% to 25% of the value of the estimated damage.

Any insurance policy proceeds should be deducted from the estimated gross value of recovery and reconstruction needs to arrive at their net value.

Housing

The housing sector is usually one of the most affected by disasters given the vulnerability of housing units to different types of hazards.

Recovery needs include the rapid construction and operation of emergency shelters and the provision of basic services for the displaced population. In some cases—particularly where the destruction of housing units has been extensive and the time to rebuild is envisaged as significantly long—transitional housing facilities and/or rental subsidies to affected families also must be provided. These costs must be estimated for each case of disaster.

In addition, the cost of replacing household goods that may have been destroyed or lost during the disaster is normally included as a recovery need for the families. The cost of such recovery need can be estimated based on a typical household set of goods as defined in the most recent household survey undertaken in the affected country, combined with unit market prices prevailing after the disaster.

Reconstruction needs are equivalent to the estimated value of damage, increased by 10%–25% to include the introduction of disaster risk reduction features in housing unit design and construction. Should it be deemed necessary, the cost of relocation to safer areas should be added to reconstruction needs. Whenever partially damaged housing units are to be repaired, their reconstruction cost should include the cost of retrofitting with risk reduction and resilience standards.

The building capacity of the construction sector should be analyzed to ascertain the probable duration of the required reconstruction program as this would have a bearing on the duration and cost of recovery needs.

After gross recovery and reconstruction needs have been estimated, the value of possible insurance proceeds should be deducted to arrive at the net value of recovery and reconstruction requirements.

Energy

In the energy sector, **recovery needs** involve the cost of several types of activities. These include, immediately after the disaster:

(i)   Cost of urgent rehabilitation works by the utility to restore power production at the source;
(ii) Cost of temporary tapping of nearby undamaged electrical grids; and
(iii) Financing of the higher-than-normal cost of electricity production from alternative power units while destroyed components of the electrical system are rebuilt (e.g., temporary use of a thermal power unit to replace a hydro or geothermal power unit).

In some cases, while electricity flows are restored by the utility, households may resort to the use of alternative sources of energy and require financial assistance for that purpose.

The cost of urgent rehabilitation works is usually met by the affected electricity utility company's use of its resources to finance the cost of labor and utilization of its inventory of spare parts and equipment. Its value can be supplied by the utility enterprise itself, so that at least the stock of parts and equipment can be replenished. The cost of a temporary interconnection line to tap electricity from nearby unaffected systems with a surplus of electricity can be provided to the PDNA team by the electric utility. Data on alternative power units may be obtained from the utility itself.

Additional recovery needs may occur whenever a temporary interconnection line may be required to tap electricity from nearby unaffected systems with a surplus of electricity. The cost of building such a temporary line can be provided to the PDNA team by the electric utility planning department or unit.

Recovery needs may also arise whenever alternative power units are required to temporarily replace electricity production in damaged units but may face a higher cost of production over the time required for reconstruction. This typical case may be illustrated whenever a thermal power unit—which has a higher cost of operation due to the use of fuel—is used to replace a hydro or geothermal power unit. Data to estimate such recovery needs may be obtained from the utility itself.

Higher costs of electricity production may be met through a temporary government subsidy, an increase in normal subsidy, or via a special credit line obtained by the utility through private banks. This measure would avoid an imbalance in the electric utility's financial governance and/or a transfer of a higher cost to consumers.

If households face a significantly higher electricity cost during recovery and reconstruction (e.g., rural households that resort to the use of wood for cooking and heating in the absence of electricity or, in the case of urban areas, where electricity rates are significantly increased), governments may introduce temporary direct cash transfers or other similar assistance schemes.

The estimation of **reconstruction needs** involves increasing the estimated value of damage to the electrical system in all its components so that an increased degree of disaster resilience is achieved. In the case of destroyed or damaged buildings, an increase of 20%–35% over damage values is considered usual. In other cases, it may be desirable to rebuild urban distribution lines underground to protect them against high winds (e.g., tropical storms), and the cost involved must be determined through a special study.

Water Supply and Sanitation

In terms of recovery and reconstruction, the water supply and sanitation sector is similar to that of energy. Recovery would be achieved when water and sanitation services are provided to the disaster-affected population with a coverage that is at least equal to that of the time before the disaster, in the same quantity and quality, and at the same rates or tariffs. In addition, reconstruction is not reached until all destroyed physical assets have been rebuilt and are operational, hopefully with disaster risk reduction and resilience standards.

A special issue to be dealt with is the recovery of institutional governance concerning the operation of systems. **Recovery needs** include the financing requirements to cover the higher-than-normal cost of operating the systems of water supply and sanitation that may occur from the time of the disaster until full recovery and reconstruction are achieved. This may entail the temporary cost of distributing water through tanker trucks, provision of bottled water, special costs of wastewater removal and disposal during the emergency, and the higher cost of bringing water from unaffected alternative sources of water during reconstruction. To ensure the financial stability of the utility, the government may be required to introduce or increase subsidies until reconstruction has been completed.

When the water utility is not able to provide sufficient water to consumers, households may resort to the purchase of bottled water and/or water purification tablets and other means at a cost that exceeds the funds available in their budget. In these cases, the government may resort to compensating such higher household expenditures through temporary social transfer schemes.

Reconstruction needs in this sector include using the estimated values of destroyed collective water and sanitation systems in urban areas and individual household or community systems in rural areas and increasing them by a factor of 10%–25% to allow for the adoption of risk-reduction features. Engineers and economists should define the rate of increase above the value of damage from the utility, depending on the post-disaster degree of resilience to be adopted. Once recovery and reconstruction needs have been estimated, any possible proceeds from insurance on assets and operations that the utility may obtain should be deducted to arrive at the net value of needs for recovery and reconstruction.

Transport

The transport sector comprises several subsectors including road, railway, and air transport, as well as related services. While these subsectors share many common features, they have some distinctive differences which have a bearing on the estimation of recovery and reconstruction needs. The destruction of physical assets—including infrastructure and vehicles—and disruptions to the availability of transport services can occur after disasters, negatively affecting the population.

Recovery needs are the amounts of financing required to restore a normal level of operation in all transport subsectors following a disaster. There are often many recovery needs:

(i)   Urgently removing blockages to traffic flows and/or the opening of alternative road sections to enable minimum traffic flows.
(ii) Setting up temporary bridges or urgent construction of fords to enable vehicular traffic over road sections where bridges or other major drainage works have been destroyed.
(iii) Establishing temporary alternative schemes of transport where normal means of transport have been destroyed or deemed unsafe.
(iv) Providing temporary government subsidies—or temporary subsidy increases—for the operation of public transport systems in urban areas to avoid possible increases in transport tariffs and rates charged to users.
(v)   Possibly providing temporary tax relief schemes for private and public transport companies.

Reconstruction needs should be estimated based on the value of damage to the destroyed physical infrastructure and on the replacement value of vehicles in public transport systems, increased to cover the cost of risk reduction features. In selected cases, the reconstruction of bridges and other major drainage works may entail additional costs relating to the adoption of enhanced standards of design to ensure adequate flood discharge capacities or earthquake resistance. In all other cases of reconstruction, the additional cost over and above the estimated value of damage may range from 12% to 25%.[7]

Once gross recovery and reconstruction needs have been estimated, the value of possible insurance proceeds should be deducted to arrive at the net value of needs.

Communications

The communications sector usually comprises postal services, telecommunications, and miscellaneous communications services. After a disaster, destruction may occur to the infrastructure and assets of these activities, followed by an interruption to or a decline in these services, as well as possible revenue losses of the private and public enterprises that operate the networks.

Recovery needs in this sector may include several cost factors. These include:

(i) urgent repair and the realignment of antennas and equipment that have sustained damage to restore a minimum flow of communications immediately following the disaster;

(ii) setting up temporary alternative communication equipment and facilities while major repairs and reconstruction works are underway;

(iii) provision of working capital through special credit lines or temporary tax exemptions to private communications companies during reconstruction, when required; and

(iv) possible government subsidies to compensate for higher-than-normal operational costs of communications enterprises to ensure the financial governance of service enterprises and to avoid an increase in consumer rates and tariffs.

Reconstruction needs refer to the replacement cost of destroyed communication infrastructure, increased by 10%–25% to include risk reduction measures and standards. Given the rapid technological development of equipment, replacement needs of equipment may involve the adoption of more recent technologies and their costs would also need to be similarly determined.

Once gross recovery and reconstruction needs have been estimated, the value of possible insurance proceeds should be deducted to arrive at the net value of post-disaster financial requirements.

7.   Estimation of Macroeconomic Recovery Needs

Following a disaster event, the value of destroyed assets and production disruption may be so high—especially in the case of small developing countries—as to cause major negative disaster impacts and macroeconomic imbalances. These may include the possible occurrence of significant negative trade and foreign currency imbalances—due to lower exports and/or higher imports—as well as high fiscal deficits due to increased expenditure and lower revenues. These, in turn, may impact the future development prospects of a country. Analysis should be undertaken to explore such potential impacts and their consequences.

When such a situation occurs, affected countries may draw on sovereign parametric insurance and insurance-linked securities if specifically based on BOP and/or balance of trade and/or fiscal balance indicators, if available.

---

[7]   This is especially true when—due to larger-than-expected flood events—the construction of a longer bridge or a change to a steel design is required.

Countries may request international assistance (e.g., from international financial institutions) to temporarily address such imbalances until the affected economy can bounce back. This type of recovery assistance may include soft-term loans to support the BOP or fiscal budget, including contingent disaster financing.

During the macroeconomic impact assessment stage of the PDNA, macroeconomic projections are usually made for several years of succeeding disasters since BOP and fiscal performance challenges can continue during reconstruction. Macroeconomic recovery needs are defined on this basis and for a multiyear period.

8.   Estimation of Personal Income Recovery Needs

Personal or household loss of income may result following a disaster causing a significant decline in productive sector output. The estimate of personal income recovery needs focuses on the vulnerable population only; that is, that part of the labor force that does not have permanent employment but, rather, is fully dependent on their income for conducting productive or trade activities. This is opposed, for instance, to government or private enterprise employees whose salaries are guaranteed despite the occurrence of the disaster.

The PDNA should obtain estimates on the value of income loss affecting the vulnerable population that lives in the disaster-affected area. Recovery of personal income for that segment of the population may be achieved through a program of cash-for-work in the reconstruction program, where workers are hired to repair or rebuild basic infrastructure or services before they can return to their normal productive activities. This kind of scheme is usually short-lived and is defined based on the expected time required to achieve sector production recovery. In some cases, these schemes are combined with food-for-work programs that may be implemented when food deficit conditions arise after a disaster.

9.   Estimation of Food Security Recovery Needs

In some disasters, food production—under crop agriculture, livestock, and fisheries subsectors—may be drastically reduced to the point where the food security of the affected population is compromised. During the PDNA, calculations of food deficits arising from a disaster should be carefully made, and possible import of foodstuffs estimated to design a temporary food security program until a balanced condition is again achieved.

When this situation occurs, and a cash-for-work or another cash transfer program is also envisaged, the food security recovery needs should be diminished by the value of the cash-for-work program to avoid duplication of assistance to the vulnerable population.

Maintenance activities of energy infrastructure in Tonga. The Cyclone Gita Recovery Project reconstructed and climate- and disaster-proofed the Nuku'alofa electricity network that was damaged by Tropical Cyclone Gita in February 2018 (photo by ADB).

Case Study

1. Introduction

As a supplement to the explanatory note on quantitative methods to estimate the recovery and reconstruction requirements within a post-disaster needs assessment (PDNA), this theoretical case study illustrates the procedures necessary to enable the quantification of the financial component.

2. Description of the Disaster and its Surrounding Areas

In May 2022, an earthquake measuring 7.2 magnitude on the Richter scale struck a country. A portion of an artificial dam providing water for the irrigation of 142,265 hectares (ha) of crops was damaged, as was the infrastructure necessary for small- and medium-sized aquaculture activities.

The dam was breached and approximately 500 million cubic meters of water (equivalent to approximately 75% of the total reservoir capacity) was discharged over a relatively brief period. An area of approximately 45,700 ha was flooded, and an estimated 70,000 people were evacuated to temporary shelters following the destruction of 5,046 homes and damage to others. Roads and ancillary drainage structures were devastated in the flooded areas and partial damage was sustained by the electricity grid(s) and water supply and sanitation network(s). Irrigation conveyance canals and related structures were also destroyed.

Rice and maize crops suffered the brunt of the earthquake and resulting flooding, which occurred during the midst of the agricultural growth calendar (Table 1).

Table 1: Agricultural Growth Calendar

Crop	2022												2023			
	Jan.	Feb.	Mar.	Apr.	May	Jun.	Jul.	Aug.	Sep.	Oct.	Nov.	Dec.	Jan.	Feb.	Mar.	Apr.
Rice																
Main			▓	▓	▓	▓	▓	▓	▓							
Second									▓	▓	▓	▓	▓			
Maize																
Main		▓	▓	▓	▓	▓										
Second							▓	▓	▓	▓						
Third									▓	▓	▓	▓	▓	▓	▓	

Source: Author.

The main rice crop and the first maize crop—which had been sown earlier in the year—were completely lost. Due to the flooding and deposition of mud, silt, and debris on the land, and the unavailability of sufficient irrigation water, the second rice crop production is forecast to be lower until remedial measures materialize. The second maize crop will not be sown, and the third maize production is also forecast to be lower until remedial measures are taken to restore soil productivity.

Aquaculture activities were suspended because of the combination of damage to its infrastructure, the loss of fingerlings, and the absence of dam water. Many domestic animals drowned, and others lost weight due to flood-induced stress and insufficient food. Some small and medium-sized enterprises (SMEs)—particularly agriculture-based industries—faced a partial production loss due to the lack of sufficient agriculture, livestock, and aquaculture production.

The effects of the earthquake and flood disaster harmed the economy of the region as well as income, food security, and the general well-being of the population. The government is currently assisting the affected population to recover from the effects and impact of the disaster.

3.   Disaster Effects

A full-fledged PDNA was conducted immediately following the emergency, which considered the social and economic sectors that were affected by the disaster. The results obtained on the values of destroyed property (damage) and values of changes in production flows of goods and services (losses) are described in this case study and are used as the basis for the quantification of recovery and reconstruction needs.

Social Sectors

Housing

After a detailed field survey, it was determined that a total of 5,407 housing units—including individual homes and apartments in multistory apartment buildings—were affected by the earthquake and flood. Of these, 5,046 units were destroyed and 361 sustained partial damage. Household goods were destroyed or rendered unusable because of the flooding from the failed dam after the earthquake.

The value of the damage was estimated by using a unit construction cost—prevailing at the time of the disaster—for individual homes and apartments in multistory buildings. The value of destroyed household goods was estimated by using the list provided in the most recent household survey, which was conducted in-country.

The cost to sanitize partially flooded housing units before reoccupation was obtained from local authorities, while that for demolishing destroyed housing units and safely removing debris and mud was estimated at 4.5% of the replacement cost of each unit. As some of the housing units were rentals, the loss in rent was recorded based on the time required for reconstruction (Table 2).

Table 2: Disaster Effects on the Housing Sector

Disaster Effects	Value of Damage and Losses ($'000)			Value by Type of Ownership ($'000)	
	Damage	Losses	Total	Private	Public
Destruction of assets	**87,991.6**		**87,991.6**	**87,991.6**	
Destroyed housing units	77,334.9		77,334.9	77,334.9	
Partially damaged housing units	5,356.7		5,356.7	5,356.7	
Destroyed household goods	5,300.0		5,300.0	5,300.0	
Change in flows		**3,495.3**	**3,495.3**	**4.6**	**3,490.7**
Rental loss		4.6	4.6	4.6	
Demolition and rubble/mud removal		3,480.0	3,480.0		3,480.0
Sanitizing damaged housing units		10.7	10.7		10.7
TOTAL	**87,991.6**	**3,495.3**	**91,486.9**	**87,996.2**	**3,490.7**

Source: Author.

Education

Information obtained during the field survey revealed that no schools were destroyed and that 26 education centers sustained partial damage because of the earthquake and subsequent flooding. School furnishings and education materials were rendered useless. Some schools were temporarily used as shelters for displaced people and subsequently sustained damage due to substantial overuse (Table 3). The affected schools were publicly owned.

Table 3: Disaster Effects on the Education Sector

Disaster Effects	Value of Damage and Losses ($'000)			Value by Type of Ownership ($'000)	
	Damage	Losses	Total	Private	Public
Destruction of assets	**5,229.7**		**5,229.7**		**5,229.7**
Partially damaged schools	4,189.0		4,189.0		4,189.0
Education equipment	207.0		207.0		207.0
Furniture	651.7		651.7		651.7
Education materials	182.0		182.0		182.0
Change in flows		**3,686.5**	**3,686.5**		**3,686.5**
Demolition and rubble/mud removal		54.0	54.0		54.0
Repair of schools used as shelters		3,632.5	3,632.5		3,632.5
TOTAL	**5,229.7**	**3,686.5**	**8,916.2**		**8,916.2**

Source: Author.

Emergency Assistance and Early Recovery for Poor Municipalities Affected by Typhoon Yolanda in the Philippines. One year after Typhoon Yolanda hit, new classrooms built in Bislig Elementary School, on the island of Leyte, are providing children with the opportunity to learn in a clean, safe environment and look forward to a better future (photo by ADB).

Health

Due to the simultaneous earthquake and flood events, various health facilities were destroyed, and others were partially damaged. In addition, furniture, medical equipment, and supplies were destroyed.

The national health system provided treatment to many of the injured. In-depth monitoring of disaster-related diseases was implemented, complemented by information and disease prevention campaigns. Buildings that were partially damaged were sanitized before reuse. Expenditures for these activities were over and above the existing government budget funding for the Ministry of Health.

Data on damage and losses were collected during various field surveys (Table 4).

Table 4: Disaster Effects on the Health Sector

Disaster Effects	Value of Damage and Losses ($'000)			Value by Type of Ownership ($'000)	
	Damage	Losses	Total	Private	Public
Destruction of assets	**1,230.2**		**1,230.2**		**1,230.2**
Destroyed health infrastructure	421.5		421.5		421.5
Partially damaged health infrastructure	514.7		514.7		514.7
Furniture	65.0		65.0		65.0
Equipment	79.0		79.0		79.0
Medical supplies	150.0		150.0		150.0
Change in flows		**256.3**	**256.3**		**256.3**
Additional medical attention		168.5	168.5		168.5
Disease surveillance and prevention		68.3	68.3		68.3
Demolition and mud/debris removal		16.9	16.9		16.9
Sanitation of damaged facilities		2.6	2.6		2.6
TOTAL	**1,230.2**	**256.3**	**1,486.5**		**1,486.5**

Source: Author.

Productive Sectors

Agriculture Crop Production

Agriculture crop production generally represents nearly 30% of the gross domestic product of the country. The dam that broke because of the earthquake was key to agriculture production, providing water for the irrigation of various crops. Due to the dam break, 19,600 ha in three adjacent districts were flooded.

Physical assets associated with irrigation and crop production were also destroyed. At the time of the disaster, farmers had already sown the first maize and main rice crops which were washed away entirely, producing an entire loss of these crops. Given the debris, mud, and silt deposited on the soil, it became impossible to sow the second maize crop, generating a full loss. Farmers—with technical and financial assistance offered by the government—undertook to remediate the soil; this included the removal of flood materials and the addition of fertilizer to enable the sowing of the second rice crop and the third maize crop. Production volume for these crops, however, was expected to be lower than normal due to a combination of insufficient irrigation water and lower soil productivity for at least the next 3 calendar years. The government undertook to finance the cost of seeds for planting the next crops (the main rice crop and the first maize crop), fertilizers, and the pumping of irrigation water from nearby sources for the following year.

The value of destroyed infrastructure was estimated by applying prevailing unit construction prices at the time of the disaster. Production losses arising from the washing away of standing crops, crops that would not be sown, and crops that would have lower unit yields in the following 2 years were also estimated (Table 5).

Table 5: Disaster Effects on the Agriculture Sector

Disaster Effects	Value of Damage and Losses ($'000)			Value by Type of Ownership ($'000)	
	Damage	Losses	Total	Private	Public
Destruction of assets	**70,517.3**		**70,517.3**	**6,252.5**	**64,264.9**
Damage to the reservoir	50,688.9		50,688.9		50,688.9
Irrigation and drainage system	13,482.4		13,482.4		13,482.4
Farm roads	6,252.4		6,252.4	6,252.5	
Other infrastructure	93.6		93.6		93.6
Change in flows		**31,664.8**	**31,664.8**	**24,685.9**	**7,002.0**
Crop production loss in 2022		21,660.1	21,660.1	21,660.1	
Crop production loss in 2023		2,252.0	2,252.0	2,252.0	
Crop production loss in 2024		750.7	750.7	750.7	
Cost of inputs for next crops		4,332.0	4,332.0		4,332.0
Cost of fertilizer		570.0	570.0		570.0
Cost of additional irrigation water		2,100.0	2,100.0		2,100.0
TOTAL	**70,517.3**	**31,664.8**	**102,182.1**	**30,915.2**	**71,266.9**

Source: Author.

Livestock

Due to flooding, livestock sustained a significantly negative impact. Many of the animals in the affected area drowned and the remainder faced significant stress. In addition, pastureland was eroded or sustained deposits of mud and debris. There was limited pasture available for livestock feed.

A count was made of the number of animals that had drowned or were missing, and the value of the damage was calculated by applying the prevailing local price of animals at the time of the disaster. Estimates of dead livestock (reflecting lower production of meat) were calculated, also based on prevailing local market prices. In addition, costs to the government for the provision of veterinary care for surviving animals that showed stress and supplementary feed to offset pastureland damage were estimated. Recovery of pre-disaster levels of meat production was forecasted to take 3 calendar years, the time necessary for a natural repopulation of livestock (Table 6).

Table 6: Disaster Effects on the Livestock Sector

Disaster Effects	Value of Damage and Losses ($'000)			Value by Type of Ownership ($'000)	
	Damage	Losses	Total	Private	Public
Destruction of assets	**929.1**		**929.1**	**929.1**	
Dead livestock	929.1		929.1	929.1	
Change in flows		**7,264.9**	**7,264.9**	**6,864.9**	**400.0**
Losses due to death of livestock		6,211.2	6,211.2	6,211.2	
Losses due to lower weight animals		403.7	403.7	403.7	
Veterinary assistance to stressed livestock		400.0	400.0		400.0
Supplemental feeding costs		250.0	250.0	250.0	
TOTAL	**929.1**	**7,264.9**	**8,194.0**	**7,794.0**	**400.0**

Source: Author.

Fisheries

Due to the failure of the dam and the partial emptying of the reservoir, most aquaculture establishments sustained the destruction of infrastructure and equipment. Furthermore, the ponds lost water and fish stock.

To estimate the value of destroyed assets, information was obtained from the fish industry association. Production losses were calculated based on the time required to repair and rebuild the dam and reservoir (7 months) as normal fisheries operations could only take place once there was sufficient pond water.

SMEs that operate within the fisheries sector require financing for the repair and reconstruction of destroyed assets. Additional financial assistance is necessary to reconstitute their working capital and to roll over outstanding nonperforming loans (Table 7).

Table 7: Disaster Effects on the Fisheries Sector

Disaster Effects	Value of Damage and Losses ($'000)			Value by Type of Ownership ($'000)	
	Damage	Losses	Total	Private	Public
Destruction of assets	**13,770**		**13,770**	**13,770**	
Destroyed ponds	12,290		12,290	12,290	
Destroyed equipment and machinery	580		580	580	
Fish stock	900		900	900	
Change in flows		**19,845**	**19,845**	**19,845**	
Production losses		14,700	14,700	14,700	
Working capital requirements		5,145	5,145	5,145	
TOTAL	**13,770**	**19,845**	**33,615**	**33,615**	

Source: Author.

Agroindustry

A limited number of physical assets of privately owned agriculture-based industries located within the flood areas were destroyed by the earthquake. These agro-based industries face future losses because of lower primary production inputs from the agriculture, livestock, and fisheries sectors due to the floods.

These processing losses will occur during the year of the disaster and the succeeding 2 years, in parallel with the primary production losses of crops, meat, and fisheries.

Data on the destruction of assets were obtained by the association of agroindustries, using the unit construction and replacement costs that prevailed at the time of the disaster. The processing losses were estimated based on primary production losses in each of the affected districts, based on the value added during the industrial process of each product. Working capital requirements for these enterprises were estimated based on a sample survey conducted during the PDNA (Table 8).

A decade since the Asian tsunami. An ADB-funded agriculture research station in Aceh, Indonesia helped revive agriculture in predominantly agrarian Aceh to reduce rural poverty (photo by ADB).

Table 8: Disaster Effects on the Agroindustry Sector

Disaster Effects	Value of Damage and Losses ($'000)			Value by Type of Ownership ($'000)	
	Damage	Losses	Total	Private	Public
Destruction of assets	**163.1**		**163.1**	**163.1**	
Damage to premises	30.2		30.2	30.2	
Destroyed equipment and machinery	18.3		18.3	18.3	
Destroyed raw materials	50.7		50.7	50.7	
Destroyed finished products	63.9		63.9	63.9	
Change in flows		**26,973.2**	**26,973.2**	**26,973.2**	
Processing losses in 2022		16,880.8	16,880.8	16,880.8	
Processing losses in 2023		2,505.3	2,505.3	2,505.3	
Processing losses in 2024		835.1	835.1	835.1	
Working capital requirements		6,752.0	6,752.0	6,752.0	
TOTAL	**163.1**	**26,973.2**	**27,136.3**	**27,136.3**	

Source: Author.

Commerce

The estimated processing loss in agroindustrial establishments (Table 8), will generate subsequent losses in the sale of processed goods as commerce is the final link in the production value chain. No destruction of the physical assets of trade enterprises, however, was recorded following the disaster.

By applying a combination of the estimated agroindustrial processing losses described in section 3.2 and the usually added value for the marketing of relevant products, losses in sales within the commerce and trade sector were estimated. As with the agroindustrial sector, full recovery of primary production will take over 3 years (Table 9).

Table 9: Disaster Effects on the Commerce Sector

Disaster Effects	Value of Damage and Losses ($'000)			Value by Type of Ownership ($'000)	
	Damage	Losses	Total	Private	Public
Sales disruption					
Loss of sales in 2022		18,339	18,339	18,339	
Loss of sales in 2023		904	904	904	
Loss of sales in 2024		301	301	301	
TOTAL		**19,544**	**19,544**	**19,544**	

Source: Author.

Infrastructure Sectors

Transport

Transport infrastructure was significantly affected by the disaster, directly and indirectly. Entire sections of inter-urban and urban roads were completely or partially destroyed, as were several bridges and ancillary drainage works. Emergency work undertaken to restore minimum traffic also resulted in surface deterioration on other roads due to the traffic of heavy machinery. Meanwhile, traffic flows were re-routed to alternative roads, causing longer time in traffic and overall higher costs of transport (Table 10).

Table 10: Disaster Effects on the Road Transport Sector

Disaster Effects	Value of Damage and Losses ($'000)			Value by Type of Ownership ($'000)	
	Damage	Losses	Total	Private	Public
Destroyed infrastructure	**39,070.0**		**39,070.0**		**39,070.0**
Roads and highways	23,811.2		23,811.2		23,811.2
Urban roads	1,469.4		1,469.4		1,469.4
Bridges	13,789.4		13,789.4		13,789.4
Partially damaged infrastructure	**27,730.0**		**27,730.0**		**27,730.0**
Roads and highways	27,730.0		27,730.0		27,730.0
Higher transport cost		**51,790.0**	**51,790.0**	**51,790.0**	
International roads		23,530.0	23,530.0	23,530.0	
Regional roads		28,260.0	28,260.0	28,260.0	
TOTAL	**66,880.0**	**51,790.0**	**118,590.0**	**51,790.0**	**66,800.0**

Source: Author.

Communications

The disaster caused partial damage to the communications sector infrastructure which, in turn, led to a loss in communications sales. Postal services infrastructure sustained minor damage, but the delivery of mail was only temporarily interrupted. Ground telecommunications facilities and cellular telephone systems were partially damaged, leading to some loss in revenue (Table 11).

Table 11: Disaster Effects on the Communications Sector

Disaster Effects	Value of Damage and Losses ($'000)			Value by Type of Ownership ($'000)	
	Damage	Losses	Total	Private	Public
Damage to infrastructure	**279.9**		**279.9**	**259.9**	**20.0**
Postal services	20.0		20.0		20.0
Telecommunication systems	259.9		259.9	259.9	
Revenue losses		**14.3**	**14.3**	**12.0**	**2.3**
Postal services		2.3	2.3		2.3
Telecommunication services		12.0	12.0	12.0	
TOTAL	**279.9**	**14.3**	**294.2**	**271.9**	**22.3**

Source: Author.

Energy

The floods caused the destruction and damage of components of the electricity system in the three affected districts. Several substations and transformers were rendered useless by the flood waters and had to be replaced, and many poles and distribution lines were knocked down and also had to be replaced. As a result, the electricity supply was interrupted in the entire flooded area, later restored in stages by the utility entity depending on the severity of the damage. Despite the relatively prompt restoration of electricity in the grid, the sale of electricity is expected to be below normal levels until damaged housing units are rebuilt and there is evidence of a recovery in the agroindustrial sector (Table 12).

Table 12: Disaster Effects on the Energy Sector

Disaster Effects	Value of Damage and Losses ($'000)			Value by Type of Ownership ($'000)	
	Damage	Losses	Total	Private	Public
Damage to infrastructure	**6,780.0**		**6,780.0**		**6,780.0**
Substations	2,510.7		2,510.7		2,510.7
Transmission lines	114.0		114.0		114.0
Distribution grid	4,155.3		4,155.3		4,155.3
Revenue losses		**709.2**	**709.2**		**709.2**
Power interruption		33.4	33.4		33.4
Lost revenue from housing sector		665.3	665.3		665.3
Lost revenue from agroindustries		10.5	10.5		10.5
TOTAL	**6,780.0**	**709.2**	**7,489.2**		**7,489.2**

Source: Author.

Water Supply and Sanitation

The earthquake and floods caused destruction and damage to physical facilities and equipment in the generation, transmission, and distribution components of water supply systems in the three flooded districts. In addition, the wastewater system in one location suffered significant damage.

Tanker trucks were made available to the three districts to distribute water to consumers for a short period, with emergency measures provided to remove wastewater in one district. The public utility is expected to face lower operational revenues over the entire reconstruction period (Table 13).

Table 13: Disaster Effects on the Water Supply and Sanitation Sector

Disaster Effects	Value of Damage and Losses ($'000)			Value by Type of Ownership ($'000)	
	Damage	Losses	Total	Private	Public
Damage to infrastructure	**12,972.0**		**12,972.0**		**12,972.0**
Water supply system	6,554.5		6,554.5		6,554.5
Wastewater system	6,417.4		6,417.4		6,417.4
Revenue losses		**48.7**	**48.7**		**48.7**
Water distribution losses		17.5	17.5		17.5
Wastewater distribution losses		31.2	31.2		31.2
TOTAL	**12,972.0**	**48.7**	**13,020.6**		**13,020.6**

Source: Author.

Building Climate Resilience of Watersheds in Mountain Eco-Regions Project in Nepal. The project is improving water management and providing water supply for use in the home and agriculture in about 100 communities in Nepal (photo by ADB).

SUMMARY OF DISASTER EFFECTS

After aggregating all sectorial values of damage and losses, the total value of disaster effects was calculated at $432 million (Table 14). Of this, $267 million represents the value of destroyed physical assets and $165 million the change in economic flows, comprising losses in the production of goods and services as well as the higher costs of production and delivery.

In terms of damage, the social, productive, and infrastructure sectors of the economy appear to have experienced a similar amount of asset destruction. In terms of production, the most affected sectors were agriculture, agroindustry, fisheries, and commerce. Transport costs increased significantly, and revenue losses negatively affected the financial position of public utilities.

Table 14: Total Summary of Disaster Effects

	Damage ($ million)	Losses ($ million)	Total ($ million)
Social sectors	**94.4**	**7.5**	**101.9**
Housing	88.0	3.5	91.5
Education	5.2	3.7	8.9
Health	1.2	0.3	1.5
Productive sectors	**85.3**	**105.3**	**190.6**
Agricultural crop production	70.5	31.7	102.1
Livestock	0.9	7.3	8.2
Fisheries	13.8	19.8	33.6
Agroindustry	0.1	26.9	27.1
Commerce	0.0	19.5	19.5
Infrastructure sectors	**86.8**	**52.5**	**139.4**
Road transport	66.8	51.8	118.6
Communications	0.3	0.0	0.3
Electricity	6.8	0.7	7.5
Water and sanitation	12.9	0.0	13.0
TOTAL	**266.5**	**165.2**	**431.8**

Source: Author.

4.   The Social Impact of the Disaster

In comparing pre- and post-disaster production figures, it was established that the personal income and food security of the population residing within the directly affected areas would sustain a significant negative impact. Government interventions would be required to assist the affected population to recover to pre-disaster levels.

Personal Income

From information on the value of pre- and post-disaster production in the three flooded districts, it was calculated that per capita gross production would decline (Table 15).

Table 15: Decline in Per Capita Gross Production

District	Per Capita Gross Product ($/person)		Decline (%)
	Pre-Disaster	Post-Disaster*	
District A	1,664,000	944,000	43
District B	633,000	273,000	57
District C	462,000	334,000	28
Entire Affected Region	1,440,000	1,341,000	7

* Projection to 2022 year-end after including production loss.
Source: Author.

Using the average total per capita income in 2021 of $806,000 for the entire region as a proxy, the total personal income in each of the three districts was estimated (Table 16). The total decline in personal income within the affected areas was estimated at $44.7 million. While this decline may be temporary, many households will inevitably fall below the poverty income threshold; the number of people experiencing poverty conditions will increase and ongoing government efforts to combat and reduce poverty will need to be increased.

Table 16: Total Personal Income

District	Estimated Per Capita Total Income ($/person)	
	Pre-Disaster	Post-Disaster*
District A	931,200	528,100
District B	354,400	152,500
District C	258,800	187,000
Entire affected region	806,000	750,500

* Estimated value for 2022 at year-end.
Source: Author.

Food Insecurity

The assessment of disaster effects revealed that food availability would significantly decline over the succeeding 3 years. The loss of crops, the decline in meat due to the death and illness of livestock and other domestic animals, and the losses in fisheries catches would generate a food deficit resulting in rising costs.

A food balance analysis would enable the quantification of an anticipated food deficit. As there is insufficient data available to assess the food balance, an estimate of the value of lost food production across all productive sectors provides an initial overview of the deficit (Table 17).

Table 17: Estimate of Food Deficit

Food Products	Value of Losses ($ million)
Agriculture food crops	21.7
Meat	6.6
Fish products	14.7
Total	43.0

Source: Author.

The $43 million in Table 17 is only an estimate of the value of food insecurity. A detailed food balance that considers pre-disaster food stocks should be undertaken to provide accuracy.

5.   Estimate of Recovery and Reconstruction Needs

The PDNA provides the necessary elements to establish the financial amounts required to achieve recovery and reconstruction following the disaster. Essentially, the amount of financing required to restore the production of goods and services across all sectors to previous levels is estimated. This should include the supply of and public access to all service sectors, as well as the reconstruction of destroyed physical assets, which should include enhanced resilience standards. The estimated values of damage and losses—as described in section 3 of this publication—should be applied together with the methodology for the systematic, and the quantitative estimate of post-disaster recovery and reconstruction needs.

Social Sectors

Housing

Recovery needs

Before the reconstruction of housing units in the flooded areas, demolition and removal of mud and debris must be undertaken. The cost for this is calculated at 4.5% of the total reconstruction, to be borne by the government.

Sanitation is required to ensure the health of the inhabitants of the partially damaged and flooded housing units. The unit cost of sanitizing is estimated at 0.2% of the total cost of repairs to damaged housing units, to be covered by government funding.

While new housing units for the affected population will be built to replace those destroyed, temporary housing facilities are necessary. The government provides temporary use of public buildings for this at no cost.[8]

Reconstruction needs

Financing is required for (i) the reconstruction of destroyed houses with enhanced disaster resilient standards at an estimated unit cost of 125% of pre-disaster levels, (ii) repairs to damaged houses including retrofitting to provide improved design standards at a similarly increased repair cost, and (iii) the replacement of household goods (Table 18).

Table 18: Recovery and Reconstruction Needs in the Housing Sector

Needs	Multiplier	Amount ($'000)
Recovery needs		**3,490.8**
Demolition and rubble removal	0.045	3,480.1
Sanitation of flooded homes	0.002	10.7
Emergency shelter costs		n.a.
Reconstruction needs		**108,664.5**
Reconstruction of housing units	1.25	96,668.6
Repairs to damaged houses	1.25	6,695.9
Replacement of household goods		5,300.0
Total		**112,155.3**

n.a. = not available.
Source: Author.

---

8   This could come at an opportunity cost and is not always available.

Education

Recovery needs

Before the reconstruction of destroyed education facilities is undertaken, full demolition is required as well as the removal of debris and rubble to areas for safe disposal. These costs can be estimated as a function (4.5%) of the total reconstruction cost.

Some schools were offered as temporary shelters to accommodate displaced families, resulting in some damage. The assessment team estimated the cost of repairs at $3.6 million.

Reconstruction needs

The cost of education unit reconstruction is estimated at 125% of the pre-disaster unit cost, which includes the introduction of disaster risk reduction and resilience standards. The replacement of destroyed equipment, furniture, and education materials is added to the total value of reconstruction (Table 19).

Table 19: Recovery and Reconstruction Needs in the Education Sector

Needs	Multiplier	Amount ($'000)
Recovery needs		**3,821.0**
Demolition and rubble removal	0.045	188.5
Repairs to schools used as shelters		3,632.5
Reconstruction needs		**6,277.0**
Reconstruction of schools	1.25	5,236.3
Replacement of education equipment		207.0
Replacement of furniture		651.7
Replacement of education materials		182.0
Total		**10,098.0**

Source: Author.

Health

Recovery needs

During the immediate aftermath of the earthquake and floods, many people were treated for injuries and disaster-related diseases at a cost over and above the regular budget of the Ministry of Health. In addition, partially damaged facilities must be sanitized before reuse and the cost of demolition and rubble removal from destroyed facilities must be met. The changes in the environment caused by floods may also result in the occurrence of vectors and further diseases. A more robust vector and other disease monitoring and control program—together with a public information campaign—is necessary.

Reconstruction needs

Infrastructure must be rebuilt with the addition of enhanced resilience standards, representing a 25% increase in the pre-disaster unit construction cost. A similar increase in the unit repair cost should be adopted for damaged infrastructure. The replacement cost of used medicines and destroyed equipment and furniture is to be added as a reconstruction need (Table 20).

The Pandemic Sub-National Reference Laboratory at the Jose B. Lingad Memorial Regional Hospital in Pampanga, Philippines, in May 2020. The laborary financed by the $3 million grant from the Asia Pacific Disaster Response Fund, can perform up to 3,000 COVID-19 tests daily, significantly increasing the country's testing capacity (photo by ADB).

Table 20: Recovery and Reconstruction Needs in the Health Sector

Needs	Multiplier	Amount ($'000)
Recovery needs		**256.3**
Demolition and rubble removal	0.045	16.9
Sanitation of damaged facilities	0.002	2.6
Additional medical attention		168.5
Disease monitoring and prevention campaigns		68.3
Reconstruction needs		**1,464.3**
Reconstruction of destroyed infrastructure	1.25	526.9
Repair of damaged infrastructure	1.25	643.4
Replacement of used medicines		150.0
Replacement of destroyed equipment		79.0
Replacement of destroyed furniture		65.0
Total		**1,720.6**

Source: Author.

Productive Sectors

Agricultural crop production

Recovery needs

Three types of recovery activities are deemed essential for the restoration of the agriculture sector to pre-disaster production levels:

(i)   government provision of inputs for the planting of rice and maize crops in place of those not harvested; farmers are not able to finance these costs;

(ii) restoration of fertility in the soils that were flooded as well as in areas where mud and silt were deposited; and

(iii) provision, through the pumping of alternative sources, of irrigation water until water levels can be restored in the failed reservoir.

Reconstruction needs

The unit cost of reconstruction of the dam and reservoir, irrigation and drainage systems components, farm roads, and other minor infrastructure is estimated to be higher than the value of the damage. Dam reconstruction stands at 145% of the original unit cost, with the remaining components at 125% (Table 21).

Table 21: Recovery and Reconstruction Needs in the Agriculture Sector

Needs	Multiplier	Amount ($'000)
Recovery needs		**7,002.0**
Cost of inputs for next crops		4,332.0
Cost of fertilizer		570.0
Cost of additional irrigation pumping		2,100.0
Reconstruction needs		**95,703.7**
Reconstruction of reservoir	1.45	71,607.9
Reconstruction of irrigation/drainage system	1.25	16,437.2
Reconstruction of farm roads		7,549.0
Reconstruction of other infrastructure		109.6
Total		**102,752.0**

Source: Author.

Livestock

Recovery needs

As a result of the flooding, many domestic animals have developed stress and are seriously prone to disease; if untreated, the animals will produce a lower amount of meat. The cost of veterinary assistance to provide the required treatment is estimated at $0.4 million.

In addition, floods have eroded much of the pasture lands in the directly affected areas, resulting in the scarcity of food for the animals. The assessment team estimates the cost of supplemental feed at $0.25 million to avert a further reduction in the production of meat and dairy products.

Reconstruction needs

Since it has been agreed that the dead livestock will not be replaced—allowing the livestock population to naturally replace itself over 3 years instead—there are no financial requirements for reconstruction in this sector (Table 22).

Table 22: Recovery and Reconstruction Needs in the Livestock Sector

Needs	Multiplier	Amount ($'000)
Recovery needs		**650.0**
Veterinary assistance for stressed		400.0
livestock supplemental feeding cost		250.0
Reconstruction needs		0
Total		**650.0**

Source: Author.

Fisheries

Recovery needs

SMEs operating with what is now a nearly empty reservoir are enduring a lack of revenue since the disaster. Nevertheless, they continue to remunerate their workers and are now devoid of working capital to recommence operations once the reservoir is refilled, which is anticipated to take place at the end of the calendar year.

An infusion of new funding should be sought from private banks, particularly in the form of soft credit. An estimation of these requirements can be made keeping in mind that the enterprises will lose $14.7 million during the time required for recovery and reconstruction.

Reconstruction needs

The cost to rebuild the destroyed ponds—while ensuring future disaster risk reduction and resilience—is estimated at 120% of the pre-disaster cost. Furthermore, it will be necessary to replace fish offspring (fingerlings) as well as the equipment and machinery that suffered damage (Table 23).

Fisheries Resource Management Project in the Philippines. Aside from fish sanctuaries, the City Government of Puerto Princesa maintains nurseries of mangrove seedlings to complement ADB's assistance through the project (photo by ADB).

Table 23: Recovery and Reconstruction Needs in the Fisheries Sector

Needs	Multiplier	Amount ($'000)
Recovery needs		**5,145.0**
Working capital		5,145.0
Reconstruction needs		**16,228.0**
Reconstruction of ponds	1.20	14,748.0
Replacement of equipment and machinery		580.0
Replacement of fingerlings		900.0
Total		**21,373.0**

Source: Author.

Agroindustry

Recovery needs

Physical assets of agroindustrial entities sustained only very minor damage. However, these enterprises will face shortages of raw materials for processing beginning in the second half of 2022 through 2024. To maintain the normal level of production, businesses will need to seek raw materials from alternative sources at higher-than-normal unit prices. As such, their financial viability potentially will be compromised, although additional amounts of working capital can be sought through bank credit, estimated at 40% of agroindustrial production losses.

Reconstruction needs

While the damage to infrastructure within the agroindustrial sector was somewhat limited, it will be essential that any reconstruction include improved standards to ensure disaster resilience. The cost is calculated at 120% of the pre-disaster unit construction cost. Moreover, any equipment and machinery that was destroyed must be replaced (Table 24).

Table 24: Recovery and Reconstruction Needs in the Agroindustrial Sector

Needs	Multiplier	Amount ($'000)
Recovery needs		**6,752.0**
Working capital requirements	0.40	6,752.0
Reconstruction needs		**54.5**
Reconstruction of destroyed assets	1.20	36.2
Replacement of equipment and machinery		18.3
Total		**6,806.5**

Source: Author.

Commerce

The commerce sector did not sustain any destruction of assets from the disaster. Furthermore, no working capital is required, given its dependence on private sector creditors.

Infrastructure Sectors

Transport

Recovery needs

The government had taken steps to immediately restore minimum traffic flows within the affected areas using regular budget funding from the Ministry of Transport.

Reconstruction Needs

The cost to reconstruct transport infrastructure—including disaster risk reduction and resilience standards— was estimated by increasing the unit costs of construction prevailing at the time of the disaster from 120% to 140%. The cost of repairs to damaged roads is included in the estimates (Table 25).

Table 25: Recovery and Reconstruction Needs in the Transport Sector

Needs	Multiplier	Amount ($'000)
Recovery needs		n.a
Urgent works to reopen minimum traffic		
Reconstruction needs		**77,371.9**
Reconstruction of roads and highways	1.20	28,573.4
Reconstruction of urban roads	1.20	1,763.3
Reconstruction of bridges and drainage works	1.40	19,305.2
Repairs to roads and highways		27,730.0
Total		**77,371.9**

n.a. = not available.
Source: Author.

Coastal Climate-Resilient Infrastructure Project in Bangladesh. New asphalt installation at an embankment is part of the improvement of the Abduler More R and H to Majhirgati GC via Kola Bazar Road (photo by ADB).

Communications

Recovery Needs

Damage to postal and telecommunication systems was minimal. Urgent repairs to restore a minimum of service were funded by public and private sector businesses from regular budget resources.

Reconstruction needs

The cost to repair postal and telecommunication system components was $279.9 million.

Energy

Recovery Needs

The cost of urgent repairs to restore a minimum flow of electricity was met by the electric utility using its budget resources. However, to restore the financial governance of the utility and to cover the lower revenues arising from the lower level of electricity consumption within the housing and agroindustrial sector, the government must increase its subsidy on a once-only basis.

Reconstruction needs

The reconstruction of destroyed assets in the electrical system requires the introduction of disaster risk reduction and resilience standards. The pre-disaster unit cost of system components will require an increase of 10% (Table 26).

Table 26: Recovery and Reconstruction Needs in the Energy Sector

Needs	Multiplier	Amount ($'000)
Recovery needs		**709.2**
Urgent repairs to restore electricity flows		-
Increase in government subsidy		709.2
Reconstruction needs		**7,458.0**
Reconstruction of assets	1.10	7,458.0
Total		**8,167.2**

Source: Author.

Water Supply and Sanitation

Recovery Needs

For the water and sanitation utility to maintain its financial governance as well as cover the cost of temporary water distribution during repair and reconstruction, it will be necessary for the government to provide a one-off subsidy increase.

Reconstruction Needs

The damaged components of water supply and sanitation systems must be rebuilt, including the establishment of enhanced resilience standards. The cost is estimated at 120% of the unit cost prevailing at the time of the disaster (Table 27).

Table 27: Recovery and Reconstruction Needs in the Water and Sanitation Sector

Needs	Multiplier	Amount ($'000)
Recovery needs		**5.9**
One-time increase in government subsidy to cover water distribution costs		5.9
Reconstruction needs		**15,566.3**
Reconstruction of water system	1.20	7,865.4
Reconstruction of wastewater system	1.20	7,700.9
Total		**15,572.2**

Source: Author.

SUMMARY OF GROSS RECOVERY AND RECONSTRUCTION NEEDS

The gross value of sectorial recovery and reconstruction needs demands is approximately $357 million (Table 28). Broken down, recovery will be around $28 million (8% of total cost), with reconstruction estimated at $329 million (92% of total cost).

Table 28: Summary of Gross Recovery and Reconstruction Needs by Funding Source
($ million)

Sectors	Recovery Needs			Reconstruction Needs		
	Public	Private	Total	Public	Private	Total
Social sectors	**7.6**	**0.0**	**7.6**	**116.5**	**0.0**	**116.5**
Housing	3.5	0.0	3.5	108.7	0.0	108.7
Education	3.8	0.0	3.8	6.3	0.0	6.3
Health	0.3	0.0	0.3	1.5	0.0	1.5
Productive sectors	**7.4**	**12.2**	**19.6**	**87.9**	**24.0**	**111.9**
Agricultural crop production	7.0	0.0	7.0	87.9	7.8	95.7
Livestock	0.4	0.3	0.7	0.0	0.0	0.0
Fisheries	0.0	5.1	5.1	0.0	16.2	16.2
Agroindustry	0.0	6.8	6.8	0.0	0.0	0.0
Commerce	0.0	0.0	0.0	0.0	0.0	0.0
Infrastructure sectors	**0.7**	**0.0**	**0.7**	**100.5**	**0.3**	**100.8**
Road transport	0.0	0.0	0.0	77.4	0.0	77.4
Communications	0.0	0.0	0.0	0.0	0.3	0.3
Electricity	0.7	0.0	0.7	7.5	0.0	7.5
Water and sanitation	0.0	0.0	0.0	15.6	0.0	15.6
Total	**15.7**	**12.2**	**27.9**	**304.9**	**24.3**	**329.2**

Source: Author.

The net value of recovery and reconstruction is estimated by deducting expected payouts on damaged and destroyed assets, and production and revenue losses under insurance policies that private and public enterprises and individuals may have. No detailed information on estimated insurance proceeds was collected during the PDNA other than what refers to the prevailing 17% penetration rate of insurance on assets in the country. This rate can be applied to the value of reconstruction and recovery to obtain the approximate net reconstruction financing requirements.[9]

A comparison must be made of the value of damage and losses during the PDNA against the value of estimated recovery and reconstruction needs. In this case, the total value of the disaster effects is around $432 million, of which approximately $267 million relates to the destruction of assets, and the balance of about $165 million represents the changes in production flows. Total gross recovery and reconstruction needs amount to $357 million, of which $329 million refers to reconstruction and $28 million represents recovery requirements.

6.   Social Recovery Needs

An analysis of the disaster impact on the social conditions of the affected population reveals a serious deterioration of living standards. As such, the government must provide the necessary interventions to ensure the stability of household income and food security.

A macroeconomic analysis relating to personal income reveals a significant decline, forcing a portion of the affected population below the poverty line. A preliminary examination of food balance demonstrates that those who were affected by the disaster will face a food deficit and insecurity at some point in 2022. While the food deficit must be accounted for as significant, there remains a need to undertake a further study of the food balance using pre-disaster food stock data relating to the affected region, to refine the results.

The deficits in personal income and food security amount to a similar significant value of about $40 million. Considering that household income and food availability derive from the same source of production and that household income finances the purchase of food, this amount can be applied as a target for social recovery. One-tenth of the total amount could be earmarked for a 3-month cash-for-work program to ensure the availability of minimum income for those families most affected, the balance of which should be applied to a food security program that will cover the affected households.

7.   Macroeconomic Balance Needs

To assist the government in maintaining its macroeconomic balance, various critical measures must take place. These relate to not only the fiscal balance but also to the balance of trade and balance of payments for the year in which the disaster occurred as well as during the entire reconstruction period.

8.   Fiscal Budget Impact

The country affected by the disaster in this case study had no parametric insurance available. The financial requirements of recovery and reconstruction therefore must be met from government fiscal resources alone (Table 29).

---

[9]   The net value of recovery and reconstruction is estimated by deducting expected payouts on damaged and destroyed assets and production and revenue losses under insurance policies that private and public enterprises and individuals may have. No detailed information on estimated insurance proceeds was collected during the PDNA. Since insurance penetration in the country is 17%, this should be used to estimate the net reconstruction financing requirement.

Table 29: Impact of Recovery and Reconstruction on Fiscal Balance
($ million)

	Without Disaster	Post-Disaster Needs	After Disaster
Revenues and grants	40,323		40,323
Current revenues	38,921		38,921
Tax revenues	36,522		36,522
Non-tax revenues	2,399		2,399
Capital revenues	711		711
Grants	691		691
Expenditures	45,067	320	45,387
Current expenditures	39,658	15	39,673
Capital expenditures	5,409	305	5,714
Current account balance	**(737)**		**(752)**
Fiscal balance	**(4,744)**		**(5,064)**

( ) = negative.
Source: Author.

Table 29 shows that following the introduction of recovery and reconstruction needs into the budget, the fiscal sector's negative current account balance will grow by 2.1%, with the negative overall fiscal balance increasing by 6.8%. It will be critical, therefore, to ensure a revision of the entire fiscal budget of the country, together with external financial support to restore the country's fiscal position to its pre-disaster level.

9.   Balance of Payments Impact

While no export crops were affected by the earthquake and floods, there nevertheless is a call for the government to cover the resulting food deficit arising from the disaster from the national food stock and/or from the importation of food. In addition, reconstruction will require construction materials from abroad, as well as the import of equipment and machinery that are not readily produced within the country. This will constitute a portion of the total cost of reconstruction, depending on the national production base of the country.

This case study has determined that the weighted average value of imported components of infrastructure construction materials represents approximately 43% of the total reconstruction cost, despite a potential variance from one sector to another.[10] The case study assumes that specialized machinery and equipment in most sectors must be imported from abroad, while much of the furniture and expendables across the board are of national origin. The total value of the imported component of recovery and reconstruction is estimated at $98.5 million.

A further issue for consideration is that due to the higher value of road transport costs, more fuel and tires will have to be imported from abroad as there is no domestic production. It has been assumed that 50% of the higher transport costs—or $25.5 million—represent the value of these imports.

On the positive side, the proceeds from insurance on destroyed private assets will provide partial relief to the balance of payments. It has been reported that some $44 million worth of insurance payouts have been projected (Table 30).

---

[10]   The weighted average value of imported component was derived by considering the necessary unit component to be imported by each sector for the reconstruction of infrastructure and for the replacement of equipment, machinery, and supplies.

Table 30: Impact of Recovery and Reconstruction Needs on the Balance of Payments
($ million per year of disaster)

	Non-Disaster BOP	Disaster Impact	Post-Disaster BOP
Goods balance	(545)		**(669)**
Exports	378		378
Imports	923	124	1,047
Services balance	**148**		**148**
Income	**(124)**		**(124)**
Current transfers	**313**	**44**	**357**
Current account balance	(208)		(288)

( ) = negative, BOP = balance of payments.
Source: Author.

In the absence of a disaster, the country had a projected balance of payments of –$208 million (in that year). However, because of recovery and reconstruction activities, an increase in imports ($124 million), and the income from insurance payouts on private assets destroyed because of the disaster, the balance of payments will reflect a 38% deficit increase of –$288 million (Table 30), in which case the country may be forced to seek international financial assistance.

A school in Rarotonga, Cook Islands. Students—beneficiaries of the Internet Connectivity Project —show off their artworks during class (photo by ADB).

www.ingramcontent.com/pod-product-compliance
Lightning Source LLC
Chambersburg PA
CBHW050057220326
41599CB00045B/7439